NIKKI G

A Portrait of Nikki Giovanni in Her Own Words

DARRYL L. LACY

iUniverse, Inc.
Bloomington

Nikki G
A Portrait of Nikki Giovanni in Her Own Words

The script contains parts of chapters 1, 2, 4 and 5 from Gemini and the following poems by Nikki Giovanni:

Cotton Candy on A Rainy Day
Ego Tripping
For Saundra
Gus (For My Father)
Mothers
My House
My Tower
Nikki-Rosa
Of Liberation
Poem for A Lady Whose Voice I Like
Poetry
Revolutionary Dreams
That Day
The Life I Led
The New Yorkers
The True Import of Present Dialogue, Black vs. Negro
When I Die

These materials were used by permission of Nikki Giovanni.

Front Cover Artwork: Tim T. Thomas

iUniverse books may be ordered through booksellers or by contacting:

iUniverse
1663 Liberty Drive
Bloomington, IN 47403
www.iuniverse.com
1-800-Authors (1-800-288-4677)

ISBN: 978-1-4759-3080-1 (sc)
ISBN: 978-1-4759-3081-8 (ebk)

Library of Congress Control Number: 2012910523

Printed in the United States of America

iUniverse rev. date: 03/14/2013

About the Author

Darryl L. Lacy was born and raised in Buffalo, New York. He earned a Bachelor of Arts degree in theater from the State University College at Buffalo and a Master of Fine Arts degree in performing arts management from Brooklyn College of the City University of New York. In 1987, he founded Darryl Lacy Productions in Harlem, New York, where he current resides.

For Michelle "Miki" Biggins

Nikki G: A Portrait of Nikki Giovanni in Her Own Words was first presented by Darryl Lacy Productions at the Harlem School of the Arts Theatre in New York City on May 12, 1990, with the following cast:

Michelle "Miki" Biggins
Estelle Johnson
Lonnie McCoy
Ava Moses
Yael Daniel M. R.
Glenn Dandridge
Brian Biggins
Michael C. Williams

Director: Darryl L. Lacy
Stage Manager: Rachel L. Ferguson

Darryl Lacy Productions presented a twentieth anniversary production of *Nikki G: A Portrait of Nikki Giovanni in Her Own Words* at the Dwyer Cultural Center in New York City on June 21, 2010, with the following cast:

Michelle Robinson
Michelle Biggins
Howard Oree Jr.
Lauren Monroe
Larry D. Hylton

Director: Darryl L. Lacy
Stage Manager: Roxy A. McCarroll

CAST
(In Order of Appearance)

Nikki	
Woman One	Mommy, Grandmother, the Program Protester, and the Blind Woman
Man One	Daddy, Grandpapa, the Dashiki Protester, and a Homeless Person
Woman Two	Gary Ann, the Church First Lady, the Flag Protester, and a Homeless Person
Man Two	The Church Soloist, the Sign Protester, A. J., and a Homeless Person

Place:
New York City
Time:
Early seventies

DIAGRAM OF SET OF NIKKI G: A PORTRAIT OF NIKKI GIOVANNI IN HER OWN WORDS

UPSTAGE

DESK

CHAIR –

BENCH

– CHAIR

TABLE

DOWNSTAGE

CHAIR

PIANO

Introduction

(A drum begins to play.
Lights slow dim up to Nikki
standing center stage.)

NIKKI
(to audience)

I was born in the Congo.
I walked the Fertile Crescent and built the Sphinx.
I designed a pyramid so tough that a star
that only glows every one hundred years falls
into the center, giving divine perfect light.
I am bad.

I sat on the throne
drinking nectar with Allah.
I got hot and sent an ice age to Europe
to cool my thirst.
My oldest daughter is Nefertiti.
The tears from my birth pains
created the Nile.
I am a beautiful woman.

I gazed on the forest and burned
out the Sahara Desert.
With a packet of goat's meat
and a change of clothes,

I crossed it in two hours.
I am a gazelle so swift,
so swift you can't catch me.
For my birthday present when he was three,
I gave my son Hannibal an elephant.
He gave me Rome for Mother's Day.
My strength flows ever on.

My son Noah built new/ark, and
I stood proudly at the helm
as we sailed on a soft summer day.

I turned myself into myself and was
Jesus.
Men intone my loving name:
All praises, all praises.
I am the one who would save.

I sowed diamonds in my backyard.
My bowels deliver uranium.
The filings from my fingernails are
semi-precious jewels.
On a trip north,
I caught a cold and blew
my nose, giving oil to the Arab world.
I am so hip even my errors are correct.
I sailed west to reach east and had to round off
the earth as I went.
The hair from my head thinned, and gold was laid
across three continents.

I am so perfect, so divine, so ethereal, so surreal
I cannot be comprehended
except by my permission.

I mean . . . I . . . can fly
like a bird in the sky . . .

(The drum stops playing.
Lights dim out)

End of Introduction

Act I

<u>Scene One</u>

(Lights up center stage left.
Nikki is seated at the desk in
her apartment.)

NIKKI
(to audience)

Childhood remembrances are always a drag
if you're Black.
You always remember things like living in Woodlawn
with no inside toilet.
And if you become famous or something,
they never talk about how happy you were to have
your mother
all to yourself and
how good the water felt when you got your bath
from one of those
big tubs that folk in Chicago barbecue in.
And somehow, when you talk about home,
it never gets across how much you
understand their feelings
as the whole family attended meetings about Hollydale.
And even though you remember,
your biographers never understand
your father's pain as he sells his stock
and another dream goes.
And though you're poor, it isn't poverty that

concerns you.
And though they fought a lot,
it isn't your father's drinking that makes a difference,
but only that everybody is together, and you
have happy birthdays and very good
Christmases.
And I really hope no white person has cause
to write about me
because they never understand
Black love is Black wealth, and they'll
probably talk about my hard childhood
and never understand that
all the while I was quite happy.

(Nikki moves downstage left)

My name is Yolande Cornelia Giovanni Jr.—after my mother.

(Lights up on center stage,
where Woman One as
Mommy is sitting in a chair.)

I remember the first time
I consciously saw her.
We were living in a three room
apartment on Burns Avenue.

Mommy always sat in the dark.
I don't know how I knew that, but she did.

That night, I stumbled into the kitchen,
maybe because I've always been
a night person, or perhaps because I had wet
the bed.
She was sitting in a chair.
The room was bathed in moonlight diffused through

2

those thousands of panes landlords who rented
to people with children were prone to put in windows.

She may have been smoking, but maybe not.
Her hair was three-quarters her height,
which made me a strong believer in the Samson myth,
and very black.

I'm sure I just hung there by the door.
I remember thinking: *What a beautiful lady.*

She was very deliberately waiting,
perhaps for my father to come home
from his night job, or maybe a dream
that promised to come by.

MOMMY
(to Nikki)

Come here. I'll teach you a poem.

> (Nikki goes to her and kneels
> next to her)

I see the moon;
the moon sees me.
God bless the moon,
and God bless me

> (Nikki returns downstage
> left)

NIKKI
(to audience)

I taught it to my son,

who recited it for her
just to say we must learn
to bear the pleasures
as we have borne the pains.

My father, Gus,
he always had pretty legs.
He swam.
Some men get those legs from tennis,
but he swam
in some sink-or-swim mud hole somewhere
in Alabama.

When he was a young man,
more than half a century ago,
talent was described by how well
a thing was done, not by whom;
that is, considering
that Black men weren't considered,
one achieved on merit.

The fact that he is short
was an idea late reaching his consciousness.
He hustled the ball on the high school court
well enough to win a college scholarship,
luckily for me,
since that's where he met my mother.

(Man One as Daddy enters
downstage right. He walks
over to Mommy. She rises
and they embrace.)

I have often tried to think lately
when I first met him.
I don't remember.

He was a stranger,
as Black or perhaps responsible fathers
are won't to be.

> (Lights out center stage as
> Daddy and Mommy exit
> upstage right.)

Nikki is the nickname given to me by my oldest sister, Gary. Gary was three years old when I was born. My dad wanted a boy, and he named her Gary Ann.

> (Lights up downstage right,
> where Woman Two as Gary
> Ann at age seven begins
> playing the piano.)

When I was a little girl, people would come up to me and say, "Nikki, can you read?" And I would proudly answer, "No, but Gary can." And they'd say, "Nikki, can you sing?" And I'd let my chest swell a bit and say, "No, but Gary can." Then they—I would imagine laughing at me, though I didn't know it then—would say, "Nikki, can you play the piano?" And I would lean back on my heels and smile as if I had this clinched too and say, "No, but Gary can!" And it really knocked me out that I knew someone who could do all those marvelous things they asked about, and sometimes someone would think to ask, "Well, what do you do?" And I'd say, "I'm Gary's sister!" If I hadn't been taught to be respectful to older people, I would have added, "Dummy." I was Gary's sister, and that really was quite enough.

> (Gary Ann stops playing.
> Lights up upstage right,
> where Mommy enters.)

MOMMY
(to Nikki)

Kim, you'll have to quit storing those rocks on the porch. Gary can fight her own battles.

NIKKI
(to Mommy)

Yes, Mommy.

> (Gary Ann resumes playing. Lights out upstage right as Mommy exits.)

I grew up protecting Gary because Gary was a lot of mouth but she wouldn't do anything.

> (At this moment, Gary Ann stops playing the piano and stands.)

GARY ANN
(to Nikki)

Kim, you know why I don't fight? It's not that I'm scared or something—but I'm a musician. What if my hands were maimed? What if I was injured or something? You understand, don't you?

NIKKI
(to audience)

And I did.

> (Gary Ann sits down and resumes playing.)

I swear I did. All I wanted from this world was to protect and nourish this great talent, who was not my cousin or best friend or next-door neighbor, but my own sister.

> (The music ends. Lights out on Gary Ann downstage right.)

I don't idolize her much anymore. As a matter of fact, our relationship hit a mature high when, in the fifth grade, she beat me up for wearing her clothes. I decided then and there we would shift to a sounder base. I would cease wearing her clothes, and she would cease beating me up. I was badder than she was anyway, so clearly I let her win. (Pause) I don't know if I'm a fighter as much as I am a basic rebel.

End of Scene One

Scene Two

> (Lights up center stage left, where Nikki is seated at her desk.)

NIKKI
(to audience)

You always think the ones you love will always be there to love you. (Pause) I didn't graduate from Austin High in Knoxville. I was an "early entrant" to Fisk University—my grandfather's alma mater. He was one of the first graduates. After my first semester, I got kicked out. I could not/did not adjust to the Fisk social life, and it could not/did not adjust to my intellect.

(Lights dim up on table
upstage right. Woman One as
Grandmother enters, escorting
Man One as Grandpapa. He
sits at the table. She sets the
table and sits.)

So Thanksgiving, I rushed home to Grandmother's without the
bitching dean of women's permission, and that dean put me on social
probation. Which would have worked, but I was very much in love
and not about to consider her punishment as anything real I should
deal with. And the funny thing about that Thanksgiving was that I
knew everything would go down just as it did. But still, I wouldn't
have changed it because Grandmother and Grandpapa would have
had dinner alone, and I would have had dinner alone, and the next
Thanksgiving, we wouldn't even have him and Grandmother and I
would both be alone by ourselves and the only change would be that
Fisk considered me an ideal student, which means little on a life scale.

(Nikki moves downstage left.)

My grandparents were surprised to see me in brown slacks and a
beige sweater, nervously chain-smoking and being so glad to touch
base again. And she, who knew everything, never once asked about
school. And he was old, so I lied to him.

(Lights out upstage right as
they dim up center stage on
two empty benches. Church
music begins. Grandmother
escorts Grandpapa to the
first bench. Nikki joins them.
Woman Two as the Church
First Lady enters from upstage
left and sits on the second
bench.)

I went to Mount Zion Baptist with them that Sunday and saw he was going to die. He just had to. And I didn't want that because I didn't know what to do about Lovenia, who had never been alone in her life.

(Man Two as the Church Soloist enters from upstage left and stands center stage and sings. After his song, the church music ends. Lights dim out center stage as Grandmother escorts Grandpapa offstage upstage right. The Church First Lady and the Church Soloist exit upstage left. Nikki crosses to downstage left.)

I left Sunday and saw the dean Monday morning. She asked if I had permission. I said I didn't need permission to go home. She said, "Miss Giovanni," in a way I've heard so long I know I'm on the right track when I hear it, and shook her head. I was "released from school" February first because my "attitudes did not fit those of a Fisk woman." Grandpapa died in April, and I was glad it was warm because he hated the cold so badly.

End of Scene Two

Scene Three

(Lights up center stage left.
Nikki is seated at her desk.)

NIKKI
(to audience)

After knocking around and sponging off my parents for a while, I went back to Fisk a woman—not a little girl just being good like everybody said.

(Lights up upstage right as
Grandmother enters. She
clears the dishes from the
table.)

My grandmother, who adored any kind of ceremony, said, "I just want to see you graduate," and I didn't know she meant it. I graduated in February 1967, and she died in March.

(Lights out upstage right as
Grandmother exits.)

My grandmother would probably have lived another ten or twenty years, but urban renewal took her home that she lived in forty-three years, and she was disjointed and lost her will to live. Like a lot of folks. I guess nobody likes to see memories paved over into a parking lot. It just doesn't show respect. I remember our finding Grandmother the house on Linden Avenue and constantly reminding her it was every bit as good as, if not better than, the old house. A bigger backyard and no steps to climb. But I knew what Grandmother knew, what we all knew. There was no familiar smell in that house. No coal ashes from the fireplaces. Nowhere that you could touch and say, "Yolande threw her doll against the wall." No smell or taste of biscuits Grandpapa had eaten with Alaga syrup he loved so much. No Sunday

10

chicken. No sound of "Lord, you children don't care a thing 'bout me after all I done for you," because Grandmother always had a need to feel mistreated. No spot in the back hall weighted down with lodge books and no corner where the old record player sat playing Billy Eckstine crooning, "What's My Name?" till Grandmother said, "Lord! Any fool know his name!" No breeze on dreamy nights when Mommy would listen over and over again to "I Don't See Me in Your Eyes Anymore." No pain on my knuckles where Grandmother had rapped them because she was determined I would play the piano, and when that absolutely failed, no effort on Linden for us to learn the flowers. No echo of me being the only person in the history of the family to curse Grandmother out and no Grandpapa saying, "Oh, my," which was serious from him, "we can't have this." Linden Avenue was pretty, but it had no life.

(Lights out on Nikki.)

End of Scene Three

Scene Four

(Lights up on Nikki standing downstage left.)

NIKKI
(to audience)

During the sixties, I considered myself a revolutionary in prerevolutionary times. Thanks to Bertha. Bertha was my roommate and a very Black person, to put it mildly. A revolutionary. Before I met her, I was Ayn Rand-Barry Goldwater all the way. Bertha kept asking, "How could Black people be conservative? What have they got to conserve?" And after awhile—realizing that I had absolutely nothing, period—I came around. So I got an afro and began the

11

conference beat and did all those Black things we were supposed to do. I even gave up white men for the Movement . . . and that was no easy sacrifice. Not that they were good—nobody comes down with a sister like a brother—but they were a major source of support for me. So when my income was terminated for ideological reasons, you'd think Bertha would say something like, "I'll take over the rent and your gas bill, since you've sacrificed so much for the Movement." You'd really think that, wouldn't you? But no, she asked me about a job. A job, for Christ's sake! I didn't even know anybody who worked but her! And here she was talking about a job! I calmly suggested that I would apply for relief. You see, I believe society owes all its members certain things like food, clothing, shelter, and gas, so I was going to apply to society, since individual contributions were no longer acceptable. She laughed that cynical laugh of hers and offered to go down with me. "No," says I, "I can do it myself." So I went down at the end of the week.

(Lights out center stage left.
Lights up downstage center,
where Nikki crosses.)

I met this old civil servant, the kind who's been there on the job since Hayes set the system up. She asked me so many questions about my personal life I thought she was interviewing me for a possible spot in heaven. Then we got to my family. I told her Mommy was a supervisor in the Welfare Department and Daddy was a social worker. She shook her head and looked disgusted—huffed her flat chest and said, "Young lady, you are not eligible for relief!" And stormed away. I started after her. "What the hell do you mean, 'not eligible'?" I said. As she turned the corner, I had to run to keep up with her. "And who are you to decide what I need? You're nothing but a jive petty bourgeois bullshit civil servant." Yes, I did. I told her exactly that. I mean, that's what she was. "Going 'round deciding people's needs! You got needs yourself. Who decides how your needs are going to be filled? You ain't God or Mary or even the Holy Ghost—telling me what I'm eligible for." I was laying her out. The

12

nerve! I'd come all the way down there and didn't have on Levis or my miniskirt but looked *nice!* I mean really *clean,* and she says I'm not eligible. Really did piss me off. At the end of the corridor she was hurrying along, I saw this figure. It was Mommy.

> (Lights up downstage right
> as Mommy enters.)

NIKKI

Don't cry, Mommy. It'll be all right.

MOMMY

Oh, Kim, why can't you be like other daughters?

NIKKI

Mom, there's going to be a Black Revolution all over the world, and we must prepare for it. We've got to determine our own standards of eligibility. That's all.

MOMMY

Oh, Kim, I love you, but why can't you just get married and divorced and have babies and things like other daughters? Why do you have to disgrace us like this?

NIKKI

But Mom, I'm broke now. All my savings are gone, and if I don't get on relief, I'll have to take a job. Oh, Mommy, what will I do if I take a job? Locked up in a building with all those strangers for eight hours every day. And people saying, "Good morning, Kim. How's it going?" or "Hey, Kim, what you doing after work?" I mean, getting familiar with me and I don't even know them! How could I stand that?

MOMMY

You'll either have to work or go to grad school.

NIKKI
(shocked)

Mom, you don't mean it. You've been talking to Bertha. You're angry with me for what I told that civil servant. I'll apologize. I'll make it up somehow. I swear! I'll get my hair done!

MOMMY
(persisting)

Kim, it's school or a job.

NIKKI

Mom, 'member when I went back and graduated from college? Magna cum laude and all. 'Member how proud you and Daddy were that I had guts to go back after all they did to me in college? 'Member what you said? 'Member how you said I had done all you wanted me to do? 'Member how you kept saying you wouldn't ask for anything else? 'Member, Mom? Mommy? 'Member?

MOMMY

Oh, Kim. Its best—really it is.

> (She hugs Nikki and exits
> downstage right. Lights out.)

NIKKI
(to audience)

My own mother turned against me. I called my father.

(Lights up upstage right, where Daddy is seated at the table)

I asked him to take me to lunch.

DADDY
(to Nikki)

What's on your mind, chicken?

NIKKI
(to audience)

He always calls me some sort of animal or inanimate object. I'm not sure what his message is.

(Lights out downstage center as Nikki crosses to table and sits.)

I didn't want to throw it on him right away.

(to him)

Daddy-Mommy-says-I've-got-to-go-to-school-or-take-a-job-and-I-don't-think-that's-fair.

DADDY

Uhumm. Would you say that again in English . . . I mean American.

NIKKI

Mommy says I have to go to school or get a job.

DADDY

Good, lambie pie. Which one is it?

NIKKI

Daddy, you don't understand. I don't think it's fair.

DADDY

Of course not, sugar lump. She shouldn't have said it like that. You just get yourself a nice job. You don't have to consider school.

NIKKI

Oh, Daddy, you're on her side, and she's been talking to Bertha, and nobody even understands me.

DADDY

I try to understand you, angel cake. I've read almost all those books on your lists and everything you've written, and I've heard all your speeches.

NIKKI

Oh, Daddy, I just wanted you to be on my side.

DADDY

Is that my name now? "Ohdaddy"? I am on your side, brown sugar. That's why I'm telling you this. Get yourself a job; then do all the things you're doing. You may readjust your methods.

NIKKI

I won't change! I won't let the bourgeois system get me!

DADDY

I didn't say your thinking, Kim. I didn't say you would readjust your *thinking*. I said you may change your *methods.*

> (Lights dim out upstage left as Nikki leaves the table and dim up center stage, where she crosses.)

NIKKI

Lunch was ruined for me. I went home to type my resume, and that wasn't easy.

> (Lights out center stage.)

> End of Scene Four

Scene Five

> (Lights up on Nikki downstage center. The other cast members join her on stage as protesters: Woman One as the Program Protester, Man One as the Dashiki Protester, Woman Two as the Flag Protester, and Man Two as the Sign Protester. They take positions at her side and behind her)

NIKKI
(to audience)

I wanted to write
a poem
that rhymes,
but revolution doesn't lend
itself to be-bopping . . .
so I thought again,
and it occurred to me
maybe I shouldn't write
at all
but clean my gun
and check my kerosene supply.
Perhaps these are not poetic
times
at all.

Dykes of the world are united.
Faggots got their thing together.
Everyone is organized.
Black people, these are the facts.
Where's your power?

Honkies rule the world.
Where your power, Black people?
There are those who say it's found in the root of all evil.
You are money.
You seek property.
Own yourself.
Three-fifths of a man,
one hundred percent whore,
chattel property,
all of us.
The most vital commodity in America
is Black people.

Ask any circumcised honkie.
There are relevant points to be considered, Black people.
Honkies tell niggers, "Don't burn.
Violence begets you nothing, my fellow Americans."
But they insist on straightened hair.
They insist on bleaching creams.
It is only natural that we would escalate.

It has been pointed out:
"If we can't outfight them, we can't outvote them."
These are relevant points to consider.
If ten percent honkies can run South Africa,
then
ten percent Black people—which has nothing to do with negroes—
can run America.
These are facts.
Deal with them.
It has been pointed out:
"The last bastion of white supremacy is in the Black man's mind."
Note—this is not a criticism of brothers.

PROGRAM PROTESTER

Everything comes in steps.
Negative step one: Get the white out of your hair.
Negative step two: Get the white out of your mind.
Negative step three: Get the white out of your parties.
Negative step four: Get the white out of your meetings.

BLACK STEP ONE:
Get the feeling out—this may be painful—endure.

BLACK STEP TWO:
Outline and implement the program.
All honkies and some negroes will have to die.
This is unfortunate but necessary.

Black law must be implemented.
The Black Liberation Front must take responsibility
for Black people.
If the choice is between the able and faithful,
the faithful must be chosen.
Blackness is its own qualifier.
Blackness is its own standard.

There are no able negroes.
White degrees do not qualify negroes to run
the Black Revolution.

The Black Liberation Front must set the standards.
There are international rules.

Acquaint yourself with the Chinese, the Vietnamese,
the Cubans,
and other Black Revolutions.
We have tried far too long to ally with whites.

FLAG PROTESTER

Remember the rule of thumb:
WILD ANIMALS CAN BE TRAINED
BUT NEVER TAMED.
The honkie is this category.
Like any beast, he can be trained with varying degrees
of excellence to
    1) Eat from the table
    2) Wash his hands
    3) Drive an automobile or bicycle
    4) Run a machine
    5) And in some rare cases has been known to speak.

This is training Black people,
and while it is amusing,

it is still a circus we are watching.
Barnum and Bailey are the minds
behind President Johnson.

You would not trust your life to a wolf or tiger,
no matter how many tricks they can learn.
You would not turn your back on a cobra,
even if it can dance.
Do not trust a honkie.

They are all of the same family.
The Black Liberation Front has free jobs to offer
for those concerned about the unemployed.
The sisters need to make flags.
There are no nations without a flag.
The Red, Black, and Green must wave from all our
buildings as we build our nation.
Even the winos have a part—they empty the bottles
which the children can collect.
Teen-age girls can fill with flammable liquid
and stuff with a rag.
Professor Neal says a Tampax will do just fine.

DASHIKI PROTESTER

Ammunition for gun and mind must be smuggled in.
Support your local bookstore.
Dashikis hide a multitude of Revolution.
Support your local dress shop.

As all reports have indicated, our young men are primary.
On-the-job training is necessary.
Support your local rebellion—
send a young man into the streets.

Our churches must bless these efforts in the name
of our Black God.
Far too long we have been like Jesus,
crucified.
It is time for the resurrection of Blackness.
"A little child shall lead them," for the Bible tells me so,
and we shall follow our children into battle.

Our choice a decade ago was war or dishonor—
another word for integration.
We chose dishonor.
We got war.

Mistakes are a fact of life.
It is the response to error that counts.
Erase our errors with the Black Flame.
We are the artists of this decade.
Draw a new picture with the Black Flame.
Live a new life within the Black Flame.

Our choice now is war or death.
Our option is survival.
Listen to your own Black hearts.

SIGN PROTESTER

Nigger,
can you kill?
Can you kill?
Can a nigger kill?
Can a nigger kill a honkie?
Can a nigger kill the Man?
Can you kill, nigger,
hun? Nigger, can you

kill?
Do you know how to draw blood?
Can you poison?
Can you stab-a-Jew?
Can you kill, hun? Nigger,
can you kill?
Can you run a protestant down with your
sixty-eight El Dorado?
That's all they're good for, anyway.
Can you kill?
Can you piss on a blond head?
Can you cut it off?
Can you kill?
A nigger can die.
We ain't got to prove we can die.
We got to prove we can kill.
They sent us to kill
Japan and Africa.
We policed Europe.
Can you kill?
Can you kill a white man?
Can you kill the nigger
in you?
Can you make your nigger mind
die?
Can you kill your nigger mind
and free your Black hands to
strangle?
Can you kill?
Can a nigger kill?
Can you shoot straight and
fire for good measure?
Can you splatter their brains in the street?
Can you kill them?

Can you lure them to bed to kill them?
We kill in Viet Nam
for them.
We kill for UN and NATO and SEATO and US
and everywhere for all alphabet but
BLACK.
Can we learn to kill WHITE for BLACK?
Learn to kill, niggers.
Learn to be Black men.

(Black out downstage center)

End of Scene Five

End of Act I

Act II

Scene One

(Lights up on upstage center, where Nikki and Man One as the Dashiki Protester are slow-dancing to music. Nikki breaks away and moves to center stage. The Dashiki Protester sings to her.)

NIKKI
(to audience)

Don't look now.
I'm fading away
into the gray of my mornings
or the blues of every night.

Is it that my nails
keep breaking,
or maybe the corn
on my second little piggy?
Things keep popping out
on my face
or
of my life.

It seems no matter how
I try, I become more difficult
to hold.
I am not an easy woman
to want.

They have asked
the psychiatrists, psychologists, politicians, and
social workers
what this decade will be
known for.
There is no doubt it is
loneliness.

If loneliness were a grape,
the wine would be vintage.
If it were a wood,
the furniture would be mahogany.
But since it is life, it is
cotton candy
on a rainy day,
the sweet, soft essence
of possibility
never quite maturing.

I have prided myself
on being in the great tradition,
albeit circus,
that the show must go on,
though in my community, the vernacular is
"One monkey don't stop the show."

We all line up
at some midway point
to thread our way through

the boredom and futility,
looking for the blue ribbon and gold medal.

Mostly these are seen as food labels.

We are consumed by people who sing
the same old song: *Stay*
as sweet as you are
in my corner,
or perhaps *just a little bit longer,*
but whatever you do *don't change, baby, baby, don't change.*
Something needs to change.
Everything, some say, will change.
I need a change
of pace, face, attitude, and life.
Though I long for my loneliness,
I know I need something
or someone
or . . .

I strangle my words as easily as I do my tears.
I stifle my screams as frequently as I flash my smile.
It means nothing.
I am cotton candy on a rainy day,
the unrealized dream of an idea unborn.

I share with the painters the desire
to put a three-dimensional picture
on a one-dimensional surface.

(The Dashiki Protester stops
singing and the music ends.
He exits. Lights out upstage
center and center stage.
Lights dim up downstage
center, where Nikki crosses.)

I used to dream militant
dreams of taking
over America to show
these white folks how it should be
done.
I used to dream radical dreams
of blowing everyone away with my perceptive powers
of correct analysis.
I even used to think I'd be the one
to stop the riot and negotiate the peace.
Then I awoke and dug
that if I dreamed natural
dreams of being a natural
woman doing what a woman
does when she's natural,
I would have a revolution.

(Lights up downstage right
and downstage left. Woman
One as the Program Protester
and Woman Two as the Flag
Protester enter downstage
right and join Nikki to sing
a song. After the song, they
exit downstage right.)

The civil rights battle had been won, and I kept seeing my generation—woman especially—losing something. So the next battle, then, is the battle for the individual. Can an individual be who she is? I'm a single woman, and I probably always will be. I had a baby at twenty-five because I wanted to have a baby and I could afford to have a baby. I didn't get married because I didn't want to get married and I could afford not to get married. I don't recommend my lifestyle for everyone. It was what I wanted at the time and I still want. I have no regrets.

(Lights up upstage right, where Mommy, Daddy, Gary Ann, and Man Two as A. J. are playing cards at the table.)

During my pregnancy, I decided to spend Labor Day with my parents in Cincinnati. We were up playing bid whist because I love bid whist and, since most of my friends are ideologists, we rarely have time for fun. I was winning when I told A. J., my brother-in-law, "I think I'll call it a day," and I went to lie down.

(Lights up on center stage left, where Nikki crosses to sit at her desk.)

GARY ANN
(to Nikki)

Are you in labor?

NIKKI

Of course not. The baby isn't coming until the middle of September.

DADDY
(to Mommy)

You better go see about Nikki. Those children don't know anything about babies.

MOMMY

They know what they're doing.

DADDY

What kind of mother are you? The baby's in pain, and all you care about is your bid!

MOMMY
(to Nikki)

Your father thinks you're going to have the baby. Are you all right?

NIKKI

Of course. I'm just a little constipated.

MOMMY

When I was pregnant with Gary, I drank beer a lot, and it helped.

> (Mommy rises from the table.)

DADDY

You're giving the baby a *BEER*? Lord, Yolande! You're gonna kill the child!

> (A. J. laughs. Mommy exits as lights dim out on upstage right and center stage left. Lights dim up upstage center and center stage. Gary Ann moves to upstage center. Nikki crosses to center stage. Gary Ann speaks while Nikki dances.)

GARY ANN

I have built my tower on the wings of a spider,
spinning slippery daydreams of paper-doll fantasies.
I built my tower on the beak of a dove,
pecking peace to a needing woman.

I have built my dreams on the love of a man
holding a nation in his palm, asking me the time of day.

I built my castle by the shore, thinking
I was an oyster clammed shut forever,
when this tiny grain I hardly noticed
crept inside and spit around
and spit around and spun a universe inside
with a black pearl of immeasurable worth
that only I could spin around.

I have borne a nation on my heart,
and my strength shall not be my undoing
'cause this castle didn't crumble
and losing my pearl made me gain
and the dove flew with the olive branch by Harriet's route
to my breast and nestled close and said, "You are mine."
And I was full and complete while emptying my womb.
And the sea ebbed . . . ohhhhhhhhh,
what a pretty little baby.

> (Lights out upstage center
> as Gary Ann walks to Nikki.
> Lights dim up upstage right,
> and Daddy and A. J. rise
> from the table and join them
> center stage.)

GARY ANN
(calling)

Mommy, we have to name Nikki's baby.

> (Mommy reenters from
> upstage right and joins the
> others center stage.)

DADDY

You know, my father's name was Thomas.

NIKKI

We'll name him Thomas.

> (Blackout on stage)
>
> End of Scene One

Scene Two

> (Lights up center stage left.
> Nikki is seated at her desk.)

NIKKI
(to audience)

Poetry is motion graceful
as a fawn,
gentle as a teardrop,
strong like the eye
finding peace in a crowded room.

We poets tend to think
our words are golden,
though emotions speak too
loudly to be defined
by silence.

Sometimes, after midnight or just before
the dawn,
we sit, typewriter in hand,
pulling loneliness around us,
forgetting our lovers and children
who are sleeping,
ignoring the weary wariness
of our own logic
to compose a poem.
No one understands it.
It never says "Love me," for poets are
beyond love.
It never says "Accept me," for poems seek not
acceptance but controversy.
It only says "I am, and therefore
I concede that you are, too."

A poem is pure energy
horizontally contained
between the mind
of the poet and the ear of the reader.
If it does not sing, discard the ear,
for poetry is song.
If it does not delight, discard
the heart, for poetry is joy.
If it does not inform, then close off the brain,
for it is dead
if it cannot heed the insistent message
that life is precious,

which is all we poets,
wrapped in our loneliness,
are trying to say.

> (Lights dim out center stage
> left and dim up center stage
> as Nikki moves there.)

A writer only has one tool, and that's herself. You are your only tool—what you think, what you feel, what you have heard, what you empathized with. You must grant integrity to even those you hate. I decided to be a writer because people said I was a genius and then would ask what I would become. And I couldn't see anywhere to go intellectually and thought I'd take a chance on feeling.

> (Lights up upstage right
> as Man Two as the Sign
> Protester enters.)

SIGN PROTESTER
(to Nikki)

You ain't got no talent.
If you didn't have a face,
you wouldn't be nobody.

NIKKI

God created heaven and earth
and all that's Black within them.

SIGN PROTESTER

You ain't really no hot stuff.
They tell me plenty sisters
take care better business than you.

NIKKI

On the third day, he made chitterlings
and all good things to eat
and said: "That's good."

SIGN PROTESTER

If white folks hadn't been under
yo' skirt and been giving you the big play,
you'd a had to come on uptown like everybody else.

NIKKI

Then he took a big, Black, greasy rib
from Adam and said, "We will call this woeman, and her
name will be Sapphire, and she will divide in four
parts
that Simone may sing a song."

SIGN PROTESTER

You pretty full of yourself, ain't chu?

NIKKI

Show me someone not full of herself,
and I'll show a hungry person.

> (The Sign Protester exits
> upstage right as lights dim
> out.)

New York is the only city where you can earn a living in the arts, but
I'm basically a midwestern girl. I write best when I'm back home.
There's a house—there's grass. I can think and dream. Here it's been

hard to adjust. Writing takes concentration. I start for my typewriter and go over to the window instead. My poetry has suffered.

(Lights out center stage.
Lights up downstage center,
where Nikki crosses. Lights
up upstage left, where Man
One, Woman Two, and Man
Two are homeless people.)

In front of the bank building
after six o'clock, the gathering
of bag people begins.

In cold weather, they huddle
around newspapers.
When it is freezing, they get
cardboard boxes.

Someone said they are rich eccentrics.
Someone is, of course, crazy.

The man and his buddy moved
to the truck stop
in the adjoining building.
Most early evenings, he visits
his neighbors awaiting
the return of his friend
from points unknown to me.
They seem to be a spontaneous
combustion, these night people.
They evaporate during the light of day,
only to emerge at evening glow
as if they had never been away.

I am told there are people
who live underground
in the layer between the subways
and the pipes that run them.
They have harnessed the steam
to heat their corner
and cook their food,
though there is no electricity,
making them effectively moles.

The twentieth century has seen
two big wars and two small ones,
the automobile and SST,
telephone and satellites in the sky,
man on the moon and spacecraft on Jupiter.
How odd to also see the people
of New York living
in doorways of public buildings
as if this is an emerging nation—
though, of course, it is.

(Lights out upstage left as
the homeless people exit.)

Look at the old woman
who sits on Fifty-seventh Street and Eighth Avenue
selling pencils.
I don't know where she spends the night.
She sits, summer and winter,
snow or raining, humming
some white religious song.
She must weight over two hundred and fifty pounds.
The flesh of her legs has stretched
like a petite pair of stockings
onto a medium frame
beyond its ability to fit.

There are tears and holes
of various purples in her legs.
Things and stuff ooze from them,
drying and running again.
There is never, though, a smell.
She does not ask you to buy
a pencil, nor will her eyes
condemn your health.
It's easy, really, to walk by her.
Unlike the man in front
of Tiffany's, she holds her pencils
near her knee.
You take or not,
depending upon your writing needs.

He, on the other hand, is blind and walking
his German shepherd dog.

His sign says, "There
but for the grace of God
goes you," and there is a long
explanation of his condition.
It's rather easy for the Tiffany shopper
to see his condition:
He is Black.

                              (Lights up downstage right,
                              where Woman One as the
                              Blind Woman enters.)

Uptown on One Hundred Twenty-fifth Street is an old, blind Black
woman.
She is out only in good
weather and clothes.

Her house is probably spotless,
as Southern ladies are wont to keep house,
and her wig is always on straight.

BLIND WOMAN
(to Nikki)

You got something for me?

NIKKI

What do you want?

BLIND WOMAN

What's yo' name? I know yo' family.

NIKKI
(laughing)

No, you don't. You don't know anything about me.

BLIND WOMAN

You that Eyetalian poet, ain't you? I know yo' voice. I seen you on
television.

> (Nikki crosses over to where
> she is standing and looks
> into her eyes.)

NIKKI

You didn't see me, or you'd know I'm Black.

BLIND WOMAN

Let me feel your hair. If you Black, hold down yo' head.

> (Nikki leans over. The Blind
> Woman touches her hair and
> laughs.)

You got something for me?

NIKKI

You felt my hair, that's good luck.

BLIND WOMAN

Good luck is money, chile, good luck is money.

> (Lights out downstage right
> and downstage center.)
>
> End of Scene Two

Scene Three

> (Lights up center stage left,
> where Nikki is seated at her
> desk.)

NIKKI
(to audience)

I know my upper arms will grow
flabby; it's true
of all the women in my family.

I know the purple veins
like dead fish in the Seine
will dot my legs one day
and my hands will wither while
my hair turns grayish white. I know that
one day, my teeth will move when
my lips smile
and a flutter of hair will appear
below my nose. I hope
my skin doesn't change to those blotchy
colors.

I want my menses to be undifficult.
I'd very much prefer staying firm and slim,
to grow old like vintage wine fermenting
in old wooden vats with style.
I'd like to be exquisite, I think.

I look forward to my grandchildren
and my flowers, all my knickknacks in their places,
and that quiet of the bombs not falling in Cambodia
setting over my sagging breasts.

I hope my shoulder finds a head that needs nestling
and my feet find a footstool after a good soaking
with Epsom salts.

I hope I die
warmed
by the life that I tried
to live.

When I die, I hope no one who ever hurt me cries,
and if they cry, I hope their eyes fall out
and a million maggots that had made up their brains
crawl from the empty holes and devour the flesh

that covered the evil that passed itself off as a person
that I probably tried
to love.

When I die, I hope every social worker in the National Security
Council,
the Interpol, the FBI, CIA, Foundation for the Development
of Black Women, gets
an extra bonus and maybe take a day off
and maybe even asks why they didn't work as hard for us
as they did
them,
but it always seems to be that way.

Please don't let them read "Nikki-Rosa." Maybe just let
some Black woman who called herself my friend go around
and collect
each and every book and let some Black man who said it was
negative of me to want him to be a man collect every picture
and poster and let them burn—throw acid on them—shit
on them as
they did me while I tried
to live.

And as soon as I die, I hope everyone who loves me learns
the meaning
of my death, which is a simple lesson:
Don't do what you do very well very well and enjoy it—it
scares white folk
and makes Black ones truly mad.

But I hope someone tells my son
his mother liked little old ladies with
their blue dresses and hats and gloves, that sitting
by the window

to watch the dawn come up is valid, that smiling at an old
man
and petting a dog don't detract from manhood.
Do
somebody please
tell him I knew all along what would be
is what will be, but I wanted to be a new person
and my rebirth was stifled not by the master
but the slave.

And if ever I touched a life, I hope that life knows
that I know that touching was and still is and will always
be the true
revolution.

(Lights out upstage center.
Lights up center stage as
Nikki moves there.)

If you got the key,
then I've got the door.
Let's do what we did
when we did it before.

If you got the time,
I've got the way.
Let's do what we did
when we did it all day.

You get the glass.
I've got the wine.
We'll do what we did
when we did it overtime.

If you've got the dough,
then I've got the heat.
We can use my oven
till it's warm and sweet.

I know I'm bold
coming on like this,
but the good things in life
are too good to be missed.

Now, time is money,
and money is sweet.
If you're busy, baby,
we can do it on our feet.

We can do it on the floor.
We can do it on the stair.
We can do it on the couch.
We can do it in the air.

We can do it in the grass,
and in case we get an itch,
I can scratch it with my left hand
'cause I'm really quite a witch.

If we do it once a month,
we can do it in time.
If we do it once a week,
we can do it in rhyme.
If we do it every day,
we can do it every way.
We can do it like we did it
when we did it
that day.

(Lights out center stage.
Lights up downstage center
as Nikki moves there.)

I only want to
be there to kiss you
as you want to be kissed
when you need to be kissed
where I want to kiss you
'cause it's my house
and I plan to live in it.

I really need to hug you
when I want to hug you
as you like to hug me.
Does this sound like a silly poem?

I mean, it's my house
and I want to fry pork chops
and bake sweet potatoes
and call them yams 'cause I run the kitchen
and I can stand the heat.

I spent all winter in
carpet stores gathering
patches so I could make
a quilt.
Does this really sound
like a silly poem?
I mean I want to keep you
warm.

And my windows might be dirty,
but it's my house,
and if I can't see out, sometimes
they can't see in either.

45

English isn't a good language
to express emotion through.
Mostly I imagine because people
try to speak English instead
of trying to speak through it.
I don't know; maybe it is
a silly poem.

I'm saying it's my house
and I'll make fudge and call
it love and touch my lips
to the chocolate warmth
and smile at old men and call
it revolution 'cause what's real
is really real.
And I still like men in tight
pants 'cause everybody has some
thing to give and, more
important, need something to take.

And this is my house, and you make me
happy,
so this is your poem.

(Lights dim out downstage
center on Nikki.)

End of Scene Three

End of Act II

End of play